Art Deco Floral Patterns
In Full Color

Art Deco
Floral Patterns
In Full Color

by
E.A. Seguy

Dover Publications, Inc.
New York

Published in Canada by General Publishing Company, Ltd.,
30 Lesmill Road, Don Mills, Toronto, Ontario.
Published in the United Kingdom by Constable and Company,
Ltd., 10 Orange Street, London WC 2.

This Dover edition, first published in 1974, is an unabridged
republication of the following two portfolios, both originally
published by Ch. Massin, Paris: *Bouquets et frondaisons: 60
motifs en couleur* (not later than 1926) and *Suggestions pour
étoffes et tapis: 60 motifs en couleur* (1927?—not later than
1928). The Publisher's Note is a new feature of the present
edition.

The plates in the original portfolios were numbered from 1
through 20; in this edition the plates from *Suggestions pour
étoffes et tapis* are numbered 21 through 40.

The first edition of this Dover publication was issued under
the title *Exotic Floral Patterns in Color*.

International Standard Book Number: 0-486-23041-4
Library of Congress Catalog Card Number: 74-77178

Manufactured in the United States of America
Dover Publications, Inc.
180 Varick Street
New York, N.Y. 10014

A 16874

Publisher's Note

In the first four decades of this century, Paris was the undisputed center of the decorative arts. Eminent painters and designers provided patterns for clothing, carpets, wallpaper. Art publishers issued a stream of stimulating portfolios. The useful and the beautiful were indissolubly wedded.

One of the most active designers during this period was E.-A. Seguy.* As early as 1902 he produced a portfolio, *Les fleurs et leurs applications décoratives*, in the Art Nouveau style then current—but already with such individuality and such a personal color sense that the portfolio is one of the outstanding manifestations of the style. In 1910 Seguy's portfolio *Textiles* was highly acclaimed. During the Twenties, when his art was at its peak, his work included *Floréal, Insectes, Papillons* (Butterflies), *Les laques du Coromandel* (versions of Chinese lacquer designs) and the two portfolios reproduced here in their entirety: *Bouquets et frondaisons* (Flowers and Foliage; 1926) and *Suggestions pour étoffes et tapis* (Ideas for Textiles and Carpets; 1927).

The 120 full-color motifs from these two portfolios are chiefly floral, though ears of maize, birds, butterflies, goldfish and fountains are also included. Striking yet exquisite colors, combined with freely flowing forms, result in a group of designs that are ideally representative of their day and look boldly forward into the art of the Thirties.

Publications by Seguy in 1931, the last year for which we have documentation, include an art journal article on the artistic possibilities of microphotographs of metal and wood, and a portfolio dedicated to crystals and similar natural forms, *Prismes*, which is one of his masterworks.

*No personal information about the artist is available, not even his dates, his Christian name or the correct form of his surname (in half of his publications it appears as Séguy, and both the accented and the unaccented forms of the name are possible). Moreover, none of his portfolios is dated. Except for the 1931 article, the dates given in this Note are approximate ones supplied by New York Public Library cataloguers.

Plate 1

Plate 2

Plate 3

Plate 4

Plate 5

Plate 6

Plate 7

Plate 8

Plate 9

Plate 10

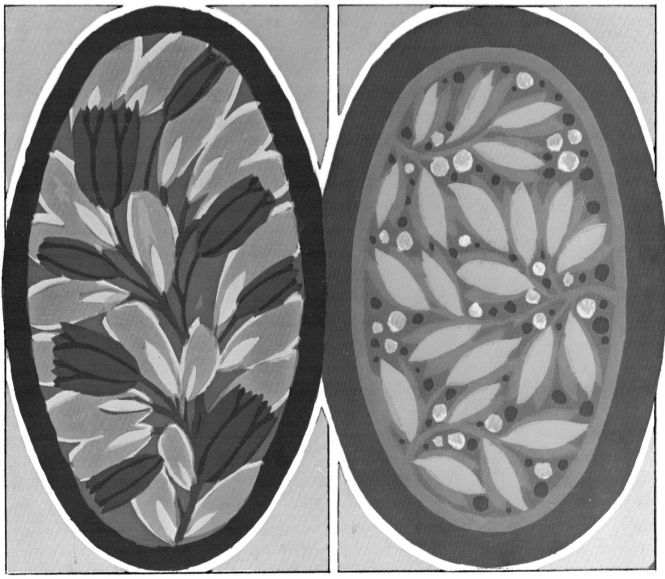

Plate 13

Plate 14

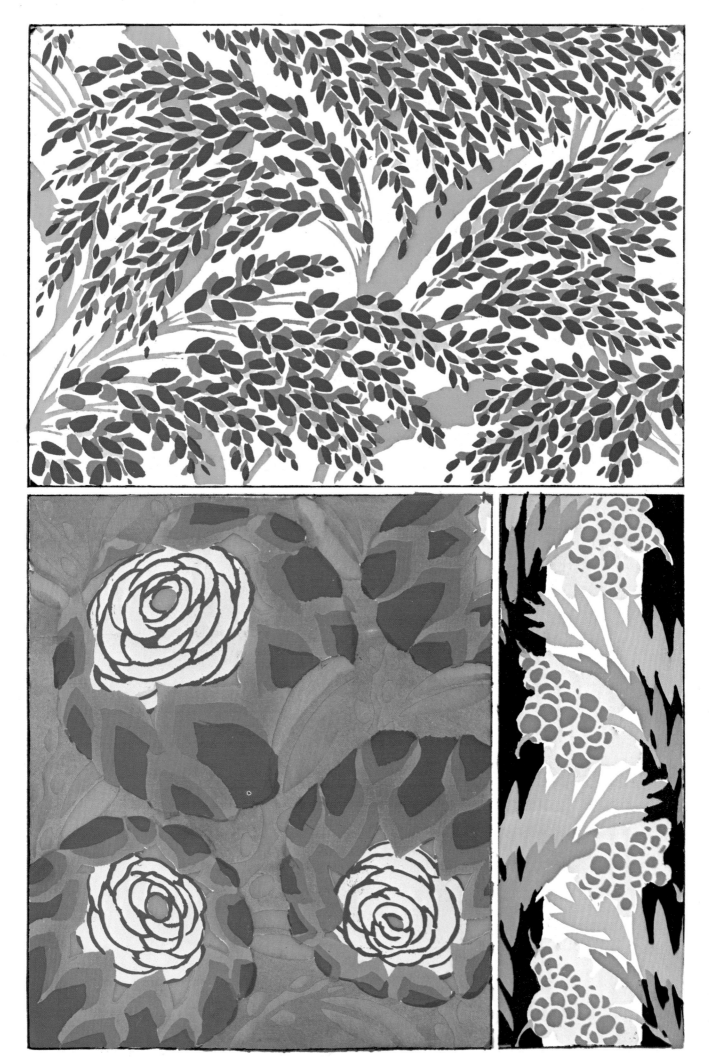

Plate 15

Plate 16

Plate 17

Plate 18

Plate 19

Plate 20

Plate 23

Plate 24

Plate 25

Plate 26

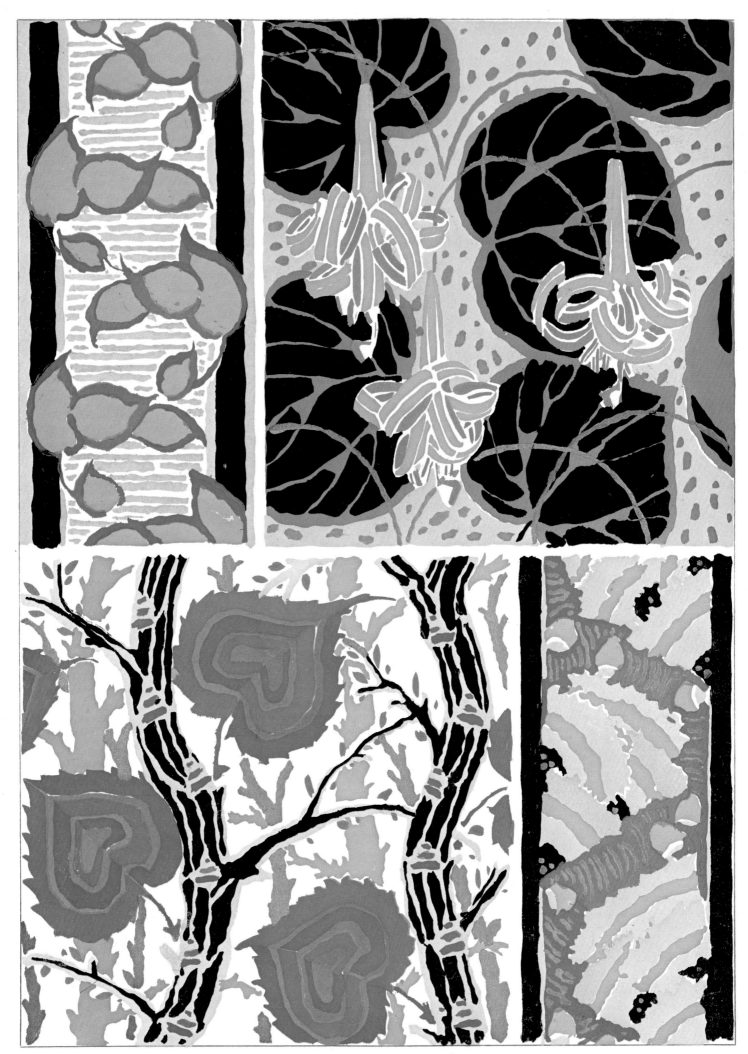

Plate 27

Plate 28

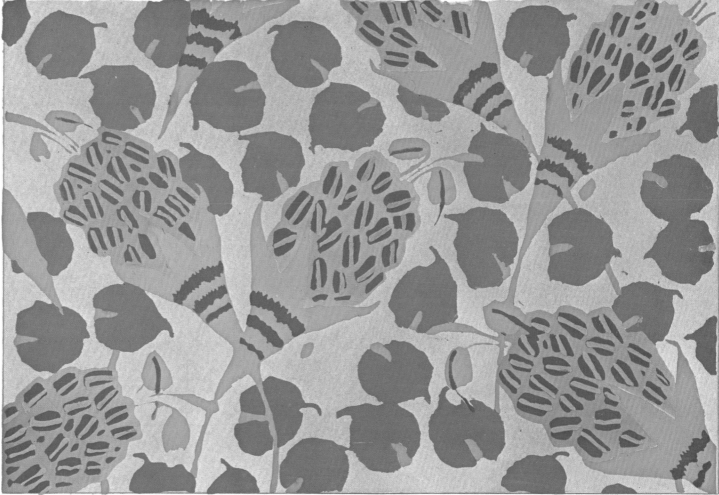

Plate 29

Plate 30

Plate 31

Plate 32

Plate 33

Plate 34

Plate 35

Plate 36

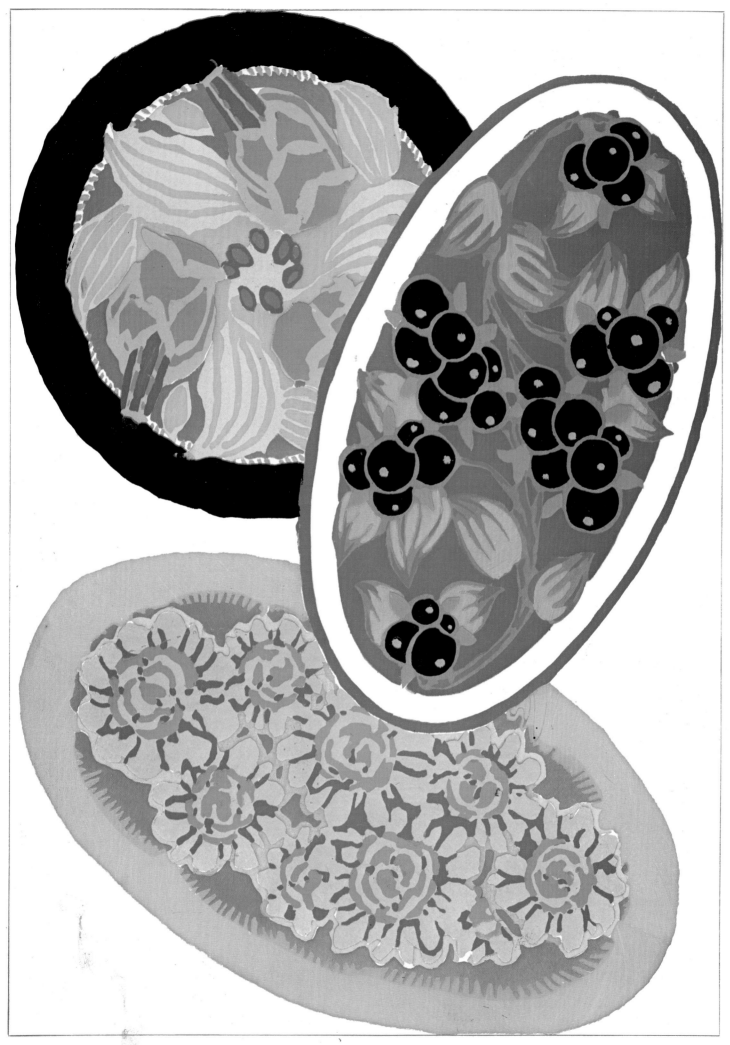

Plate 37

Plate 38

Plate 39

Plate 40